Explore
ANTARCTICA

Explore the Continents

Bobbie Kalman & Rebecca Sjonger

🌲 **Crabtree Publishing Company**

www.crabtreebooks.com

Created by Bobbie Kalman

Dedicated by Rebecca Sjonger
To Richard and Nicole Matthews, the best neighbours ever

Editor-in-Chief
Bobbie Kalman

Writing team
Bobbie Kalman
Rebecca Sjonger

Substantive editor
Kelley MacAulay

Editors
Molly Aloian
Michael Hodge
Kathryn Smithyman

Photo research
Crystal Foxton

Design
Katherine Kantor

Production coordinator
Heather Fitzpatrick

Prepress technician
Nancy Johnson

Consultant
Emma J. Stewart, Ph.D Student and Trudeau Scholar,
Department of Geography, University of Calgary

Illustrations
Barbara Bedell: pages 14, 18, 21 (krill and whale), 30
Katherine Kantor: pages 4 (map), 5, 8 (top), 20, 22
Robert MacGregor: front cover (map), back cover (map), pages 6, 7, 8 (bottom),
    10, 15 (map), 16 (map), 19 (map), 26 (map)
Vanessa Parson-Robbs: pages 17, 25 (bottom), 27
Bonna Rouse: pages 4 (starfish), 16 (seal and starfish), 21 (seal), 25 (top)
Margaret Amy Salter: front cover (snowflakes), pages 4 (penguin),
    12 (snowflakes)

Photographs
© Ann Hawthorne/Arcticphoto.com: pages 24-25
© CanStockPhoto.com: page 9
Corbis: © Bettmann: page 22; © Graham Neden/Ecoscene: page 28
© Oleg Ivanov/Fotolia.com: page 14 (ice)
Minden Pictures: Colin Monteath/Hedgehog House: page 27
Photo Researchers, Inc.: J.G. Paren: page 11
SeaPics.com: © Bryan & Cherry Alexander: page 30; © Ingrid Visser: page 23
© Emma J. Stewart: pages 26, 31 (top)
Image courtesy of Michael Studinger, Lamont-Doherty Earth Observatory
    of Columbia University: page 14 (continental ice sheet)
Visuals Unlimited: Fritz Polking: pages 12-13
Other images by Digital Vision and Eyewire

Library and Archives Canada Cataloguing in Publication

Kalman, Bobbie
    Explore Antarctica / Bobbie Kalman & Rebecca Sjonger.

(Explore the continents)
Includes index.
ISBN 978-0-7787-3071-2 (bound)
ISBN 978-0-7787-3085-9 (pbk.)

    1. Antarctica--Geography--Juvenile literature.
I. Sjonger, Rebecca II. Title. III. Series.

G863.K34 2007   j919.8'9   C2007-900585-3

Library of Congress Cataloging-in-Publication Data

Kalman, Bobbie.
    Explore Antarctica / Bobbie Kalman & Rebecca Sjonger.
        p. cm. -- (Explore the continents)
    Includes index.
    ISBN-13: 978-0-7787-3071-2 (rlb)
    ISBN-10: 0-7787-3071-9 (rlb)
    ISBN-13: 978-0-7787-3085-9 (pb)
    ISBN-10: 0-7787-3085-9 (pb)
    1. Antarctica--Juvenile literature. I. Sjonger, Rebecca. II. Title.
    III. Series.
    G863.K35 2007
    919.8'9--dc22
                                                    2007002707

Crabtree Publishing Company

www.crabtreebooks.com   1-800-387-7650

Published in Canada
Crabtree Publishing
616 Welland Ave.
St. Catharines, Ontario
L2M 5V6

Published in the United States
Crabtree Publishing
PMB16A
350 Fifth Ave., Suite 3308
New York, NY 10118

Published in the United Kingdom
Crabtree Publishing
White Cross Mills
High Town, Lancaster
LA1 4XS

Published in Australia
Crabtree Publishing
386 Mt. Alexander Rd.
Ascot Vale (Melbourne)
VIC 3032

Contents

Oceans and continents

Earth is made up of water and land. Three-quarters of Earth is covered by water. The largest areas of water are called **oceans**. There are five oceans on Earth. From largest to smallest, they are the Pacific Ocean, the Atlantic Ocean, the Indian Ocean, the Southern Ocean, and the Arctic Ocean.

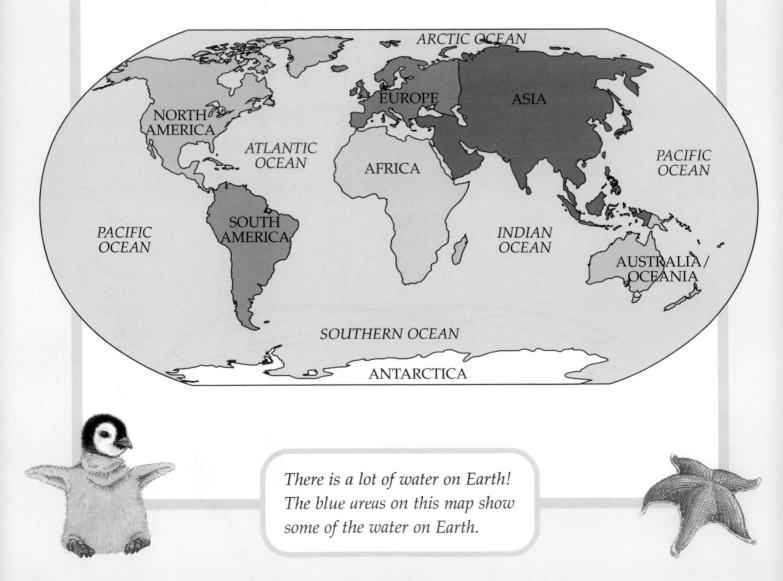

There is a lot of water on Earth! The blue areas on this map show some of the water on Earth.

Seven continents

There are seven **continents** on Earth. Continents are huge areas of land. From largest to smallest, the continents are Asia, Africa, North America, South America, Antarctica, Europe, and Australia/Oceania.

Fast fact

There is ocean water all around two continents. Antarctica and Australia/Oceania have water around them.

Four directions

There are four main **directions** on Earth. North, south, east, and west are the four main directions. The most northern place on Earth is the **North Pole**. The most southern place on Earth is the **South Pole**. In areas near the North Pole and the South Pole, the weather is cold year round.

N
W←⊕→E
S

EQUATOR

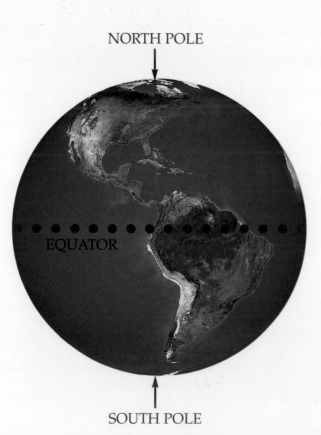

NORTH POLE

EQUATOR

SOUTH POLE

The equator

The **equator** is an imaginary line around the center of Earth. It divides Earth into two equal parts. In areas near the equator, the weather is hot all year long.

The Northern Hemisphere

The **Northern Hemisphere** is the part of Earth that is between the equator and the North Pole.

ANTARCTICA

The South Pole is at the bottom of Earth. It is in Antarctica.

The Southern Hemisphere

The **Southern Hemisphere** is the part of Earth that is between the equator and the South Pole. Antarctica is in the Southern Hemisphere.

Welcome to Antarctica!

Antarctica is the most southern continent on Earth. In Antarctica, the weather is almost always freezing cold. The land is covered in ice and snow. The cold Southern Ocean surrounds Antarctica. There are also **seas** around Antarctica. A sea is a small area of ocean water with land around it.

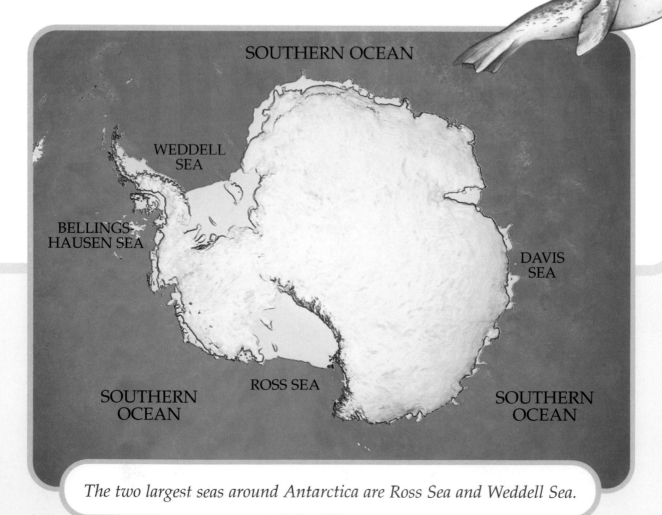

SOUTHERN OCEAN

WEDDELL SEA

BELLINGS-HAUSEN SEA

DAVIS SEA

ROSS SEA

SOUTHERN OCEAN

SOUTHERN OCEAN

The two largest seas around Antarctica are Ross Sea and Weddell Sea.

No countries

Antarctica is the only continent without **countries**. A country is a part of a continent. A country has **borders** and a **government**. Borders are areas where one country ends and another country begins. A government is a group of people who make decisions for a country. Antarctica does not have a government. The governments of countries in other continents make decisions for Antarctica (see pages 24-25).

Light and dark

Earth moves in a circle around the sun. It takes one year for Earth to move once around the sun. Earth is tilted. For half the year, Earth is tilted so that the Southern Hemisphere is pointed toward the sun. For the rest of the year, Earth is tilted so that the Southern Hemisphere is pointed away from the sun.

TILT OF EARTH

NORTHERN HEMISPHERE

EQUATOR

SOUTHERN HEMISPHERE

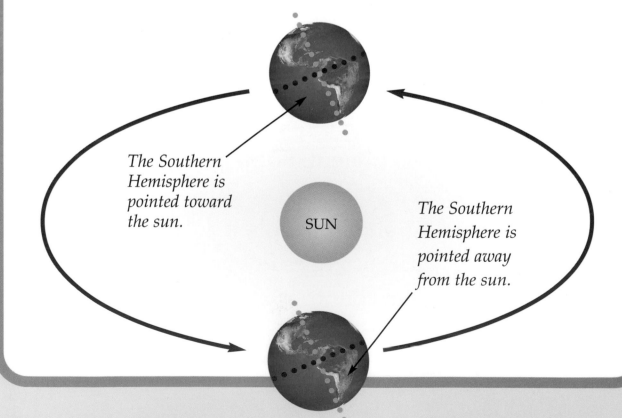

The Southern Hemisphere is pointed toward the sun.

SUN

The Southern Hemisphere is pointed away from the sun.

Day or night?

When the Southern Hemisphere is pointed toward the sun, Antarctica gets a lot of sunlight. The sun shines day and night for six months! When the Southern Hemisphere is pointed away from the sun, Antarctica gets very little sunlight. It is dark both day and night for six months.

This picture shows Antarctica when the Southern Hemisphere is pointed toward the sun. It is nighttime, but the sun is still shining!

Cold continent

Climate is the weather conditions that a place usually has. Weather includes wind, rain, snow, and temperature. Antarctica has a cold climate all year long because it is far from the equator. Antarctica has two main seasons. It has a very long winter and a very short summer.

Dry and windy

Antarctica is very dry. Most of the continent gets almost no rain. Each year, a little snow falls. All year, freezing winds blow across the continent. The winds blow the snow into the air. The blowing snow creates storms called **blizzards**.

Penguins have thick feathers. The feathers keep penguins warm during blizzards.

Covered by ice

Almost all of Antarctica is covered by very thick ice. This thick ice is called the **continental ice sheet**. In most places, the continental ice sheet is over one mile (1.6 km) thick!

Fast fact
There is enough ice in the continental ice sheet to make over thirteen million ice cubes!

Ice shelves

In some places, the top of the Southern Ocean freezes into huge sheets of ice. The ice sheets float on the ocean. Sometimes the ice freezes against parts of Antarctica's **coast**. A coast is the part of land that touches an ocean or a sea. A sheet of floating ice that is frozen onto land is called an **ice shelf**.

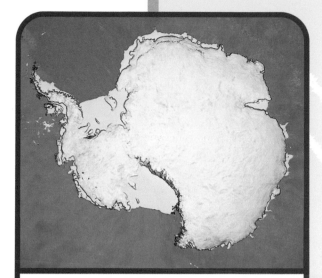

The light blue areas on this map show ice shelves. The ice shelves are along parts of Antarctica's coast.

ice shelves

Ross Ice Shelf is on the coast of Antarctica. It is in Ross Sea. Ross Ice Shelf is the world's largest ice shelf.

Antarctic lands

There are many **mountains** in Antarctica. Mountains are high areas of land that have steep sides. They are a kind of **landform**. Landforms are areas of land that have different shapes.

Mountains in the middle

The Transantarctic Mountains are a huge **mountain range** in the middle of Antarctica. A mountain range is a line of mountains. These mountains split Antarctica into two halves—the eastern half and the western half.

Transantarctic Mountains

There are also some islands in Antarctica.

ANTARCTIC PENINSULA

EASTERN HALF OF ANTARCTICA

WESTERN HALF OF ANTARCTICA

The Antarctic Peninsula

There is a large **peninsula** on the western part of Antarctica's coast. A peninsula is land that sticks out into water and is joined to a larger piece of land. The peninsula in Antarctica is called the Antarctic Peninsula.

Many kinds of penguins and seals spend time on the Antarctic Peninsula.

Very few plants

Only a few plants are able to grow in Antarctica. Most plants need sunlight and water to grow. Antarctica is dark for half the year and gets only a little rain! The plants that grow in Antarctica are called lichens, mosses, and algae. They grow along the coast. These plants grow only in summer, when some of the ice melts.

Fast fact

Antarctica is the only continent where trees do not grow!

There are very strong winds in Antarctica. Antarctic plants grow close to the ground so the strong winds will not blow them away.

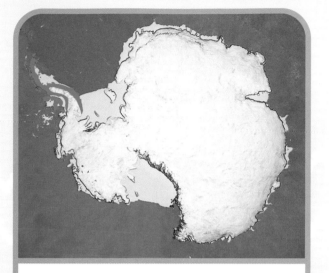

The green areas on this map show where most Antarctic plants grow in summer.

Peninsula plants

Most plants in Antarctica grow on the Antarctic Peninsula. During summer, the Antarctic Peninsula is warmer than the rest of Antarctica. One reason the peninsula is warmer is that it is a little closer to the equator than the rest of Antarctica is.

These plants are growing on the Antarctic Peninsula.

Antarctic animals

Very few animals can live on land in Antarctica. The climate on the land is too cold, too dry, and too windy for most animals. Insects are the only animals that live on Antarctica all year long. Some **sea birds** spend part of their time on land in Antarctica.

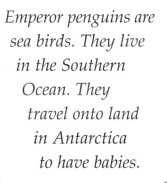

Emperor penguins are sea birds. They live in the Southern Ocean. They travel onto land in Antarctica to have babies.

Busy waters

Many animals live in the Southern Ocean around Antarctica. Millions of tiny animals called krill live there. Most other animals in the Southern Ocean eat krill. Weddell seals, crabeater seals, and humpback whales are some of the animals that eat krill.

Weddell seal

krill

Animals on the go

Some animals live in the Southern Ocean only in summer. In winter, this ocean is too cold for most animals. Before winter begins, the animals swim north. They swim to the Pacific Ocean or the Atlantic Ocean. The waters of these oceans are much warmer.

Humpback whales live in the Southern Ocean only during summer.

Exploring Antarctica

Hunters discovered Antarctica about 200 years ago. Soon after, **explorers** from many countries traveled to Antarctica. Explorers are people who travel to places to learn new things about them. Many explorers wanted to be the first to reach the South Pole.

On December 14, 1911, a Norwegian explorer named Roald Amundsen and his team were the first people to reach the South Pole. Amundsen is the man holding the camera.

Killing too many!

The hunters who discovered Antarctica were looking for fur seals. People thought of fur seals as **natural resources**. Natural resources are things found in nature that people sell to make money. People made seal fur into clothing, which was sold. Hunters killed almost a million fur seals in Antarctica in only a few years! They also killed thousands of other animals in the Southern Ocean. Finally, some people realized that the animals in Antarctica needed protection. If the animals were not protected, they might all be killed.

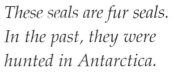

These seals are fur seals. In the past, they were hunted in Antarctica.

The Antarctic Treaty

In 1959, twelve countries from around the world signed the **Antarctic Treaty**. A treaty is an agreement made by two or more countries. The countries that signed the Antarctic Treaty agreed to set up rules that protect the continent's land and animals. For example, one rule states that people cannot fight wars in Antarctica. Antarctica is protected so that scientists can do **research** there. Research is studying something to learn more about it. Some scientists in Antarctica research the land and the animals.

The flags of the first twelve countries to join the Antarctic Treaty are still flying at the South Pole.

The treaty today

Today, 45 countries have signed the Antarctic Treaty. Some of these countries are the United States, Canada, Russia, the United Kingdom, and Norway. The 45 countries make sure that all countries around the world follow the rules of the Antarctic Treaty.

Fur seals are now protected by the Antarctic Treaty.

Protecting resources

The Antarctic Treaty has rules that protect Antarctica's natural resources. For example, people are no longer allowed to hunt animals in Antarctica. People also cannot dig in the ground for natural resources such as gold. Digging for resources would destroy the places where animals live.

The Patagonian toothfish lives in the waters around Antarctica. Many people used to fish for it. Today, it is protected by the Antarctic Treaty.

People in Antarctica

About 4,000 people live and work in Antarctica every summer. Only about 1,000 people stay in winter. Most of these people are scientists. Scientists do research there. They live in groups of buildings called **research stations**. There are 58 research stations across Antarctica. People no longer work in some of these stations, however.

Several research stations in Antarctica are shown on this map. The name of the country that owns the research station is in brackets after the station's name.

This research station is called Scott Base. It is owned by New Zealand.

Tourists in Antarctica

Each year, almost 30,000 **tourists** visit Antarctica. Tourists are people who travel to places to have fun. Many tourists in Antarctica also want to learn about the continent. **Tour companies** take tourists to Antarctica. The tour companies make sure that the tourists they take to Antarctica will not hurt the animals or damage the land.

Tourists watch the animals of Antarctica, such as this humpback whale. They also visit the camps of famous explorers.

27

Global warming

Many scientists in Antarctica are studying **global warming**. Global warming is the warming of Earth and its oceans. Burning **fuels**, such as coal and oil, is one cause of global warming. People burn these fuels to run their cars and to heat their homes.

*This scientist is releasing a **weather balloon**. Scientists use weather balloons to find out if some areas in Antarctica have become warmer.*

Flooding the land

Global warming causes the climate to become warmer. When the climate gets warmer, the ice in Antarctica starts to melt. If too much ice melts, the oceans around the world will have a lot more water. More ocean water will cause the coasts of every continent to be flooded.

Cool it!

People can help Antarctica by reducing global warming. They can ride bikes instead of driving cars. They can turn off lights and computers that they are not using. If people do these things, fewer harmful fuels will be burned.

As Antarctica gets warmer, large pieces of ice shelves break off into the Southern Ocean.

Postcards from Antarctica

Antarctica is one of the most unusual places on Earth! Thousands of tourists travel to this icy continent every year. Here are some of the things people can see in Antarctica.

The Dry Valleys are areas between the Transantarctic Mountains. These areas are a lot like Mars! Scientists study the valleys to learn more about Mars. Many tourists also visit the Dry Valleys.

Sir Ernest Shackleton explored Antarctica in 1907. He built this hut at Cape Royds, Antarctica. He lived in the hut for part of the two years that he spent exploring Antarctica. Today, many tourists visit Shackleton's Hut at Cape Royds.

Icebergs are huge chunks of ice. They float in the Southern Ocean around Antarctica. Penguins and seals rest on the icebergs.

Glossary

Note: Boldfaced words that are defined in the text may not appear in the glossary.

Antarctic Treaty An agreement made by many countries stating that Antarctica remain a peaceful place for scientific research

blizzard A storm that has strong winds and blowing snow

continental ice sheet A very thick sheet of ice that covers most of Antarctica

fuel A material, such as oil or coal, which is burned to create power

island An area of land that is completely surrounded by water

research station A group of buildings in which people live and do research

sea bird A bird that spends most of its time around oceans

tour company A company that takes tourists on trips to far away places

weather balloon A balloon scientists send into the air to get information about the temperature and wind in an area

Index

Printed in the U.S.A.